Introduction

Situated at the edge of the Salisbury Plain military training are[a] villages of Codford St Mary and Codford St Peter turned alm[ost] during the two World Wars. During WWI the surrounding Wyl[ye] them, while Codford had a total of fifteen camps. In Septem[ber] portion of the New Kitchener's Army is coming to this district f[or] than 24,000 will arrive in the neighbourhood of Codford where they will be encamped for this purpose.'

In July 1916 it was decided to open a New Zealand Infantry base unit in England and Codford became the New Zealand Command Depot. Command Depot was a term used to distinguish depots specially devoted to the reception of unfit men from the ordinary Infantry or General Base depots where reinforcements and fit men were in training to go to the Front. The Royal Army Medical Corp hospital on 'the Punchbowl', a deep cleft in the Downs just off the Chitterne Road, was taken over by the New Zealand Medical Corps and became known as No 3 New Zealand General Hospital with about 300 beds.

Across Church Lane is the Commonwealth War Grave [ANZAC] Cemetery, the final resting place of a single British soldier buried with 66 New Zealanders and 31 Australians from WWI and a lone Welsh Guardsman from WWII. In St Mary's churchyard there are the graves of two local men who died in WWII as well as soldiers of the Great War and one from the Victorian Wars who came to train and never left. In the church there is a War Memorial to ten local men who died while on active service.

These 120 men were more than names inscribed on a memorial or a grave, they should never be forgotten. This book tells something of their stories.

Romy Wyeth

1st March 2013.

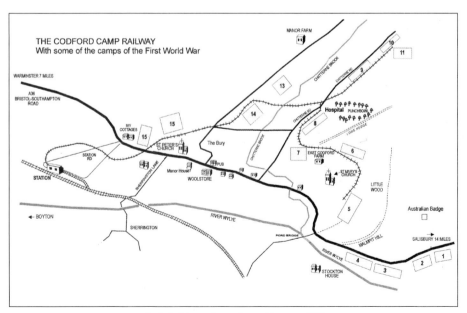

The Codford Camp railway and some of the camps of WWI.   *Brian Marshall.*

The Men of St Mary's
World War I

Private 23129 Albert Frederick Ward

Twenty-one year old Albert Ward was the first and the youngest to fall in battle. He was born at Sturton Caundle near Sherborne in Dorset and enlisted in the 10th [Service] Battalion Gloucestershire Regiment at Warminster. The Battalion was formed at Bristol as part of the 3rd New Army shortly after war was declared. It was in the role of Army Troops, attached to and administered by HQ 26th Division which was based in Codford. They moved first to Codford in September 1914 when the Division was formed. Then, when the weather broke they moved to winter billets in Cheltenham returning to Codford in April 1915. The Battalion landed in France on 6th August 1915.

Albert Ward died on 25th September 1915, the first day of the Battle of Loos [Artois III.] On that day the 10th Glosters attacked a German trench line in the Noyelles-Hulluch-Puits area of France from Le Rutoire north west of Loos. There were only 130 survivors from the Battalion; many of the casualties, including Private Ward were unlisted. He is buried in St Mary's A. D. S. Cemetery at Haisnes. At the time of his death his father Ernest Joseph Ward was living at 26 Chitterne Road, Codford St Mary.

There were 50,000 British casualties at the Battle of Loos, the highest number of British casualties ever experienced to that date.

Rifleman R/2784 Arthur Francis Simper

Arthur Simper enlisted in Warrington and served as a rifleman in the 12th [Service] Battalion King's Royal Rifle Corps. The Battalion, part of the Second New Army [K2] formed at Winchester and trained at Bisley, Blackdown, Hindhead [in billets] and finally at Larkhill until April 15th before going to France [Boulogne] on 22nd July 1915. His parents George and Eliza Simper lived at 8 Riverside, Giggin Street, Codford St Mary. George was a blacksmith who married Eliza Shears in 1883, they had five children, Arthur Francis, born in 1895, was the youngest. In the1911 Census he is registered as an apprentice draper.

Arthur died of wounds 13th February1916 and his name is between panels 51-53 on the Ypres Menin Gate Memorial in Belgium that bears the names of 54,000 officers and men whose graves are not known.

Private 265988 Archie Arthur Portingale

Archie was in the 7th [Service] Battalion Somerset Light Infantry. He was born at Monkton Deverill in Wiltshire and enlisted in Warminster, initially serving with the Wiltshire Regiment. At the time of his death his parents Edmond and Elizabeth lived at 33 Cheapside, Codford St Mary. Archie was the youngest son and he didn't want to go to war. He was eighteen at the outbreak of war but did not enlist with the early rush of enlistments possibly being conscripted sometime early in 1917. After initial training he was sent as a reinforcement to the 7th Somerset Light Infantry, which had been on active service in France and Belgium since 30th May 1915.

He was twenty-two years old and had been in France for two to three weeks when he was killed on 16th August 1917, the very first day the 7th Battalion engaged in the Battle for Langemark, part of the Third Battle of Ypres, the opening moves of what evolved into the Battle of Passchendaele. Although the battle was judged a success for the Battalion it suffered severe casualties,

Archie Portingale

over forty men were killed, one hundred and forty-eight were wounded and eighteen other ranks were missing. He is remembered in The Golden Book of Remembrance in Wells Cathedral and on Panel 41-42 of the Tyne Cot Memorial, Passchendaele, Belgium.

Corporal 14131 Albert Edgar Read

Albert Read was born and enlisted in Salisbury and was killed in action either in France or Flanders. He served with 'D' Battery, 71st Brigade Royal Field Artillery -this formed part of 15th Scottish Division, a Kitchener's New Army Division and was in France from July 1915 remaining in action on the Western Front for the rest of the war.

Forces War Records and the Commonwealth War Graves Commission lists his death as 29th April 1917 when the Division and 71st Brigade were in action in the Battle of Arras-first battle of the Scarpe, whilst the Royal Artillery Historical Trust lists his date of death as 19th April 1918. Albert is commemorated on the Arras Memorial MR20 Bay 1.

Private 6558 Arthur Charles Pond

Arthur Pond was born in July 1890 at Sutton Parva in Wiltshire, the son of William and Marie Pond. At the time of his death his parents lived at Middle Farm, Codford St Mary. Arthur was brought up a Baptist and had gone to Emwell House Private School in Warminster. He served three years in the Wiltshire Yeomanry before emigrating at the age of twenty-three to Australia, settling in Perth, Western Australia and working as a farm labourer.

Army Form B, 103.-11.
Part II.

M.R.   **(SERVICE AND CASUALTY FORM Part II).**

Regiment Corps ___11th Bn. 21st Reinfts___   Regimental Number _6558_
*Substantative Rank ___Pte___ Surname ___POND___ Christian Names _Arthur, Charles_
*Acting Rank_____
(* To be entered in pencil to facilitate alteration.)

| | | (A) Report | (B) | (C) Record of promotions, appointments, reductions, casualties, transfers, postings, &c. All acting as well as substantive promotions to be shown, for method of entry of which see A.C.I. 1816 of 1917. Corps and unit to which transferred and posted to be invariably named. | (D) Place of casualty | (E) Date of promotion, reduction, reversion, casualty, &c. | (F) Remark initials and of an e |
		Date.	From whom received.	Authority of Part II. of Orders				
1.		OC.Tps.		A.23 "Suffolk" Emb.	F'mantle	10/10/16	
2.				Disembarked	P'mouth	2/12/16	
3.		2/12/16	OC 8th Tng Bn	M/in from Aus.		2/12/16	D05
4.		19/12/16	OC. 3rd Tng Bn	M/in from Aus.		17/12/16	D05
5.		2/2/17	CO.3rd Tng Bn	Proceeding O/Seas ex Folkestone per SS "Victoria"		4/2/17	D08E
6.		4/2/17	1st ADBD	Joined Base Depot	Etaples	4/2/17	
7.		7/2/17	"	Struck off strength	"	7/2/17	
8.		23/2/17	CO. Bn.	Joined Batt.	Field	10/2/17	D01
9.		30/3/17	"	To Hosp	"	26/3/17	D01
10.		30/3/17	3rd A.F.Aust. 1 DRS	Adm. Bronchitis	"	29/3/17	
11.		31/3/17	45th CCS.	"	"	29/3/17	
12.		7/4/17	"	"	"	29/3/17	
13.		3/4/17 -	5th Gen Hosp.	"	"	3/4/17	
14.		14/4/17	5th Gen	To Con Depot	"	13/4/17	
15.		"	2nd Con Depot	Adm. "	"	13/4/17	
16.		15/4/17		Classified T.B. to B.I.D.	Etaples	14/4/17	
17.		21/4/17	1st ADBD	Joined Base Depot	"	18/4/17	
18.		24/4/17	"	Struck off strength	"	21/4/17	
19		26/4/17	C/O Bn.	Rejoined Batt	Field	21/4/17	D02
20.		11/5/17	CO.11th Bn		France	6/5/17	D028
		18/5/17	"	Now reported not missing, but wounded in action	"	6/5/17	D029

(Left margin: To be folded on this line. / Nothing to be written in this margin. / W.185y.-PP.1130 5000.00 5/18 G.W.P.Co.(3490))

3

(A) Report		(B) Authority of Part II. of Orders	(C) Record of promotions, appointments, reductions, casualties, transfers, postings, &c. All acting as well as substantive promotions to be shown, for method of entry of which see A.C.I. 1816 of 1917. Corps and unit to which transferred and posted to be invariably named.	(D) Place of casualty	(E) Date of promotion, reduction, reversion, casualty, &c.	(F) Remarks, and initials and rank of an officer
Date.	From whom received.					
21. 12/5/17	5th	F.Amb.	Adm. BW right arm	France	6/5/17	
22. 12/5/17	3rd	CCS.	"	"	6/5/17	
23. 7/5/17	7th	Con Gen	Adm. BW right arm	"	7/5/17	
24. 19/5/17	"	"	To 6th Con Dep.	"	19/5/17	
25 22/5/17	6th	Con Dep.	Adm. & Transf to 5th Con Dep.		20/5/17	
26. 22/5/17	5th	"	Adm. "	"	22/5/17	
27. 8/6/17	"	"	Transf to B D.	"	8/6/17	
28. 16/6/17	1st	ADBD	Joined Base Depot	"	9/6/17	
29. 13/6/17	"		M/out to unit	"	13/6/17	
30. 16/6/17	C/O	11th Bn	Rejoined Batt	Field	15/6/17	D034/4351
31.		CO.11th Bn	With Unit		7/2/18	
32. 8/6/18		"	Sick to Hosp	Field	27/5/18	D049/3124
33. 27/5/18	3rd	A.F.Amb.	Adm. influenza	"	27/5/18	
34. 1/6/18	17th	CCS.	" "	"	1/6/18 D	
35. 5/6/18		"	Discharged to duty	"	5/6/18	D046/2919
36. 23/6/18	CO.11th Bn		Rejoined from Hosp	"	8/6/18	
37. 17/8/18	"		Killed in action	France	10/8/18	D068/4841

(SIGNED) D. R. CROOKS. CAPT.
FOR OFFICER I/E RECORDS.

AUSTRALIAN SECTION. 3rd ECHELON G.H.Q.
B. E. F.

Nothing to be written in this margin.

Arthur enlisted in Perth, Western Australia on 10th June 1916 and was with the 11th Battalion, 21st Reinforcement Australian Imperial Force arriving at Portsmouth on 2nd December 1916. He is listed as joining the Battalion in the field in France on 23rd January 1917; on 26th March he was admitted to hospital with bronchitis, re-joining the Battalion on 21st April. Arthur was briefly reported missing in action on 6th May; he had a bullet wound in the right arm. On 27th May 1918 Arthur was back in hospital this time with influenza, he was discharged from hospital on 5th June and killed in action by a bullet on the 10th August 1918. Arthur was twenty-eight when he died and is recorded as being buried by his comrades at a location about 2,500 yards south of Herleville. Arthur was one of the 10,885 members of the Australian Imperial Force killed in France with no known grave. He is remembered on the Australian Memorial at Villiers-Bretonneaux.

Private 45197 Herbert Poolman

Herbert Poolman was born in Codford where he lived with his wife at 53 Codford St Mary. He enlisted seven miles away in Warminster and served with the 2nd Battalion Durham Light Infantry. Given his age it is possible he may have already been a soldier, the DLI records indicate he was previously with the West Riding Regiment. The 2nd Battalion arrived in France, at St Nazaire as part of the original British Expeditionary Force on 10th September 1914. Herbert died of 'illness' on 27th August 1918 aged thirty-one and is remembered on the Special Prisoner of War Memorial at Valenciennes [St Roch] Communal Cemetery, Nord. Every officer from the 2nd Battalion who was taken prisoner was captured on 21st March 1918 so it is likely that Herbert was taken at the same time. On that day they were at Beugnatre as part of the Brigade Reserve.

Valenciennes was in German hands from the early part of the war until the 1st/2nd November 1918 when it was entered and cleared by the Canadian Corps. The POW Memorial was erected to commemorate nineteen soldiers from the UK who died as prisoners of war; nine are buried in Valenciennes and ten in Le Quesnoy. None could be identified so they are remembered in both places.

Private 200495 W. George Portingale

George Portingale died in Palestine, thirteen months after his younger brother Archie, on 19th September 1918, the day Jerusalem fell to the Allies, and is buried in Ramleh War Cemetery. Like Archie he was born in Monkton Deverill, his next of kin details list him as the husband of Mrs Maclean [formerly Portingale] of 4 Carpenters Arms Yard, Trowbridge. George was serving with the 1st/4th Battalion Wiltshire Regiment who were in the front line with the 2nd/3rd Ghurkhas on the 19th September during the capture of El Tirah. During this action three officers were killed, six officers wounded [one of whom died of wounds the next day], sixteen NCOs and men killed and sixty-two wounded.

George Portingale
(right of photograph)

Private 152634 George Elliot Grant

George Grant was born in Amesbury in 1885, the second youngest of the six children of Thomas and Mary Grant. In 1891 Thomas was working as a shepherd and living with his family in Chitterne Road, Codford St Mary. Ten years later the Grants still lived in Chitterne Road, now young George was the under shepherd. By 1911 his parents had moved to Cheapside, Codford, George was now living with the family of Jacob Woods at Idminston near Salisbury and was working as a farm carter.

He enlisted at Basingstoke and served with the 50th Battalion Machine Gun Corps [Infantry], he may have previously been Private 18429 Hampshire Regiment. The machine gunners were nicknamed 'The Suicide Club' as they were the target of every enemy weapon. George was probably one of a six man detachment; two men were needed to carry the equipment, since the gun and tripod together weighed forty- eight and a half pounds. Two more men were needed to carry the ammunition, leaving two spare men. In The Great War 170,500 officers and men served in the MGC of whom 62,049 became casualties; George Grant was one of them. He died aged 33 on 23rd October 1918 and is buried in Quietiste Military Cemetery [initially known as 'Farm Cemetery'], Le Cateau, France. His next of kin is listed as his wife Elizabeth living in Wherewell, near Longparish, Hampshire.

Corporal 456041 William John Arthur Davis

William was the son of Mr J.A. & Mrs H. Davis of 31 Chitterne Road, Codford St Mary. He was born in Westbury, Wiltshire and enrolled in 231st Field Ambulance Royal Army Medical Corps. The 231st Field Ambulance Corps was the result of an amalgamation on 14th January 1917; William was probably a member of the 2nd South Western Mounted Brigade Field Ambulance when it merged with the Welsh Border Mounted Brigade Field Ambulance, both of the Territorial Force, serving at the time in Palestine.

After the Battle of Tell Asur between 8th-12th March 1918 the 74th Yeoman Division to which the 231st F.A.C. belonged were hastily redeployed as reinforcements to France to counter the massive German March 1918 Offensive, which had almost ended the War in Allied Defeat. They became part of the Western Frontier Force concentrated around Rouen in France. The German offensive had been halted with extreme difficulty and heavy casualties with both sides exhausted. The battles and engagements of the Division that autumn were the Second Battle of Bapaume 2nd-3rd September, the battles of the Hindenburg Line 12th - 24th September, the battle of Epehy 18th September and the Final Advance in Artois and Flanders 3rd October - 11th November. It appears that William Davis was twenty-seven when he died of wounds eleven days before the Armistice on 31st October 1918. He is buried in Tournai Communal Cemetery, Allied Extension, Hainaut, Belgium.

Private G. Penny (Wilts Territorials) -It has been difficult to identify this soldier. The balance of probability is that he is:.
Lance Corporal 9188 Henry George Penny
Henry George Penny was born in 1893 in Stockton, the eldest surviving child of Henry Robert and Emily Penny. In 1911 his father was a groom on a Stockton farm, with seven sons and a daughter living at home. 18 year old Henry was working as a carter on the farm. He was living in Tisbury when he enlisted in the 2nd Battalion Duke of Edinburgh's [Wiltshire Regiment] in Salisbury. Henry was one of the reinforcements rushed to the Battalion after the disaster at Reutel 22nd-24th October 1914 when over 500 men were captured by the Germans. He was killed in action on 12th March 1915 in the Battle of Neuve Chapelle. He has no known grave but is remembered on Panel 33-34 Le Touret Memorial.

Soldiers graves St Mary's Churchyard.

Private 3297 Neal McCourt
Was a twenty-five-year-old militia man who died of sunstroke in the intense heat of July 14th 1876 at Steeple Langford. He was with the Irish Militia, the Louth Rifles training of Salisbury Plain during the period of the Victorian Wars. Neal McCourt was from Seatown, Dundalk, he gave his occupation as a railway cleaner when he enrolled in the Louth Rifles on Christmas Eve 1872.

Private 15670 William Cooper
Twenty year-old William Cooper's gravestone was erected by the officers and men of the 10th [Service] Battalion Cheshire Regiment in token of their sincere regrets. He had been training in Codford for about two weeks when he collapsed and died at a 9.30am church parade on 27th September 1914. Witnesses called at the Inquest at Manor Farm Dairy said that he was a man of pretty robust health, but that he had complained of 'a dizziness in the head' about 7.30am when he was on watch that morning. He had risen at 5am and before the parade he had gone into the village for a breakfast of bacon and eggs.
As the soldiers got into line William Cooper suddenly fell backward, he was carried away and laid on the ground, it was thought he was suffering from apoplexy as he was moving in an agitated way. He died about seven minutes later. The Coroner determined that the cause of death was asphyxia suffocation due to an epileptic fit.

Lance Corporal 13795 George Fenn
This is a WWI Commonwealth War Grave in the churchyard at the eastern end of the church. Lance Corporal Fenn died on 1st June 1915 while serving in the 7th Battalion The Bedfordshire Regiment. George Fenn was born in Hotwells in Gloucestershire and was a resident of Bristol at the time he joined the Army. From his service number it appears that he enlisted around 9th September 1914 in Bristol. The Regiment, nicknamed The Shiney Seventh, was formed in Bedford September 1914, moved to Salisbury Plain May 1915 and left for France in July 1915. The cause of death is unknown.

At the south east corner of the churchyard are five men who died between 25th October 1915 and 13th February 1916, only the last man has a cause of death listed as pneumonia.

Private 17/564 A.C. Short
Private Short who died on 25th October 1915 served in the 17th [Service] Battalion Northumberland Fusiliers. They were raised in Hull in September 1914 by the North Eastern Railway Company. The Battalion was at Codford from 21st August 1915 remaining as War Office Troops till they landed at Le Havre in France 21st November 1915. They eventually took on an unusual role for an Infantry Battalion by becoming GHQ Railway

Construction Troops.

Private 4129 J. McEwan
Private McEwan died on 26th December 1915. He was with 4th/5th Battalion Lancashire Fusiliers, formed in Southport as a home service depot or training unit in the spring of 1915, moving to Codford shortly after.

Gunner L/17062 K. Marsh
Gunner Marsh was with the Royal Field Artillery when he died on 5th January 1916.

Gunner L/17006 William Smith
William Smith was serving with the 32nd Division Ammunition Column, Royal Field Artillery when he died on 14th January 1916. The Divisional Ammunition Column totalled 23 personnel, they were responsible for transporting all ammunition, both artillery and small arms for the Division.

Serjeant 4125 C. Whitehead
Serjeant Whitehead was serving with the 3rd/8th Battalion Manchester Regiment when he died aged 33 of pneumonia on 13th February 1916 . He was the son Henry and Annie Whitehead who were living at 79 Cheadle St, Higher Openshaw, Manchester and was the husband of Annie Whitehead [nee Ellis].

Private 14260269 Ben Sheppard
Ben aged 20 was living at 45 Chitterne Road; he was an apprentice blacksmith at Sutton Veny and a member of the Codford Home Guard when he enlisted in the 1st Battalion The Duke of Wellington's Regiment [West Riding] in 1940. He probably sailed from Africa to the Battalion in Italy in December 1943 and was launched onto the Anzio Beachhead in January 1944. At some stage during the fierce fighting at Anzio Ben was wounded in the shoulder while pulling a dead friend from a machine gun. He was evacuated to England by hospital ship. During the voyage his wound turned gangrenous and he died on 11th March 1944 in Cambridge Military Hospital, Aldershot. Ben Sheppard was buried in St Mary's Churchyard, Codford.

Ben Sheppard

Leading Aircraftsman 1468187 Thomas Robert Stacey
Tom Stacey was born on the 14th February 1903 in Hackney, London the fifth son of a police officer. Shortly after his birth his parents Charles & Eliza Stacey moved to a farm in Chitterne eventually settling in 58 High Street, Codford where they opened a general store and newsagents. He was 38 when he volunteered to join the Royal Air Force in September 1941, after training he served as an aircraft gunner. He took part in the North African Campaign moving on to Italy then returning to Egypt for a few months late1943 or early 1944. After which he returned to England. He was stationed at Old Sarum just outside Salisbury before being posted to RAF Eshott, a training airfield 20 miles north of Newcastle.

On 7th March 1945 Tom was mustered to a fire-fighting unit. Official records state '1468187 Leading Aircraftman Thomas Stacey was with 54 Operational Training Unit at RAF Charter Hall, 15 miles South west of Berwick on Tweed. On 30th May he was tragically killed when his fire tender overturned on the perimeter track.' On the night he died Tom was on fire tender duty having swapped shifts with a friend when the crew were called out to an emergency. He is buried close to Ben Sheppard in St Mary's churchyard.

Tom Stacey (Right)

Codford St Peter Churchyard
Private 5543 F.E. Tullett
This single war grave in St Peter's is a soldier of the 8th [Service] Battalion East Surrey Regiment who died on 12th July 1915. The Battalion was formed in August 1914 at Kingston on Thames as part of Kitchener's Second New Army in August 1914 then were sent to Purfleet to join the 55th Division. In April 1915 they moved to Colchester and then onto Salisbury Plain. Sixteen days after Private Tullett died on 28th July, the Battalion landed at Boulogne.

Suvla Bay Gallipoli

8

The Origins of ANZAC

At the outbreak of the First World War Australia and New Zealand were both quick to offer support to Great Britain. Thousands of volunteers from all over Australia and New Zealand eagerly enlisted. The offer of help was readily accepted by Britain and in early 1915 a force of five infantry divisions and one light division were provided by Australia, and one infantry division was provided by New Zealand.

They sailed for the Greek island of Lemnos to be made ready for the Gallipoli campaign.

At 0400 hours on 25th April 1915, the ANZAC Corps were put into long boats so they could be landed at dawn. The intention of the commanders was to land the ANZACs at the lowlands below Suvla Bay, but a strong tide and current forced the initial landing to be misplaced and the force landed facing steep cliffs and well defended Turkish positions. Despite this the Turks were forced back – due only to the grim determination, aggressive fighting spirit and outstanding courage displayed by previously 'unblooded' troops.

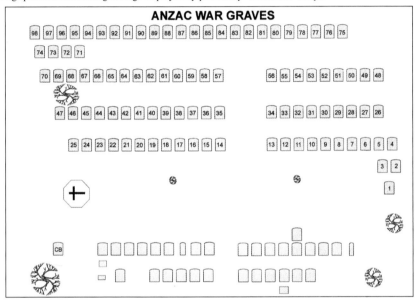

Map of Commonwealth War Grave Cemetery by Brian Marshall

The ANZACs fought continuously and improved their position until the campaign was abandoned nine months later. Of the original force landed, 66 per cent were killed or wounded. The morale of those fine men was never broken and they strongly resented being withdrawn. Since then, 25th April has been set aside as a national holiday, when Australians and New Zealanders remember those men and women of all three services who fell in all wars.

The Commonwealth War Grave [Anzac] Cemetery
Church Lane, Codford St Mary, Wiltshire

A small plot of land in a tranquil corner of the village close to St Mary's Church was established as a Military Burial Ground by deed of gift after the Great War. Planted with Irish Yews and Beech trees the ANZAC Cemetery is under the auspices of the Commonwealth War Grave Commission. It is the largest New Zealand War Grave Cemetery and the second largest ANZAC War Grave Cemetery in the United Kingdom. The plot contains 1 British soldier, 66 New Zealanders and 31 Australians from WWI and a lone Welsh Guardsman from WWII. Wiltshire burial grounds are the last resting place of 636 soldiers and airmen of the Australian Imperial Force and 173 members of the New Zealand Expeditionary Force.

Inside the hedge from Beanis Path is a single grave, directly behind it two more; there are three rows of graves with an aisle in the centre; four individual graves and finally a long row along the western boundary. These are the ANZAC graves; the WWII headstone is beneath a tree to the east of the Cross of Sacrifice.

1] **Fletcher, Pte 7455 Harry David** 13th Bn. Australian Infantry. Died 29th July 1917. Enlisted Sydney, New South Wales.

2] **Harris, Pte 640 Albert Arthur** 4th Coy Australian Machine Gun Corps. Died of wounds 27th July 1917 aged 23. Son of Arthur and Eliza Harris of Ranelagh, Tasmania. [a]

3] **Patience, Pte 7795 Frank Nicholas,** 16th Bn. Australian Infantry. Died of pneumonia 27th October 1917 aged 19. Son of Joseph and Elizabeth Patience of Georgina, Western Australia; born in Greenough.

4] **Couchman, Pte 2881 Arthur John** 51st Bn. Australian Infantry. Died of broncho-pneumonia 15th February 1917 aged 30. Widowed mother Mrs S. M. Couchman of North Fremantle, Western Australia; enlisted Fremantle 10th July 1916; born Dartford, Kent, England; worked as a labourer.

5] **Williams, Pte 6859 James Thomas** 16th Bn. Australian Infantry. Died of influenza and cardiac failure 18th February 1917 aged 29. Son of Mr J.M. & Mrs M.E. Williams of Kalcuddering, Kounongorring, Western Australia; born at Goomalling; was a farmer before enlisting in Toodyay, WA.

6] **McIlroy, Pte 6607 Gabriel** 15th Bn. Australian Infantry. Died of bronchitis 19th February 1917 aged 39. Son of Patrick & Ann Christina McIlroy; a gold miner born at Charters Towers, Queensland.

7] **Flanagan, Pte 6762 John Richard** 16th Bn. Australian Infantry. Died of pneumonia 19th February 1917 aged 43. Son of Luke & Annie Flanagan; a civil servant born at Tatura, Victoria.

8] **Morton/ Lessells Pte 6809** [served as John Morton –true family name John Macindish Adamson Lessells] 15th Bn. Australian Infantry. Died 19th February 1917. Enlisted Brisbane, Queensland.

9] Bickley, Pte 6852 Thomas George 16th Bn. Australian Infantry. Died of bronchitis 23rd February 1917 aged 37. Son of Absolon & Mary Bickley; husband of Rose Bickley of Wagin, Western Australia; born at Fremantle; worked as a labourer.

10] McGrath, Pte 7026 James Charles Patrick 15th Bn. Australian Infantry. Died of pneumonia 2nd March 1917 aged 21. Son of Patrick & Margaret McGrath of St Lawrence, Rockhampton, Queensland; enlisted St Lawrence; schooled at home; worked as a station hand.

11] Gorman, Pte 6019 Thomas Michael 15th Bn. Australian Infantry. Died of sickness 14th March 1917 aged 25. Son of Patrick John & Mary Gorman; born at Brisbane, Queensland; enlisted Petrie Terrace, Queensland.

12] Connelly, Pte 3144 Percy Francis 49th Bn. Australian Infantry. Died of pneumonia 19th March 1917. Enlisted Banalow, New South Wales.

13] Holder, Pte 7251 Harry 16th Bn. Australian Infantry. Died of cerebrospinal meningitis 28th April 1917 aged 32. Son of Harry & Grace Leggo Holder of 109 St Leonard's Avenue, West Leederville, Western Australian; born in Cornwall, England, emigrated to Australia apparently with his family when he was 27; worked as a farmer. Six brothers enlisted, Harry's younger brother John Leggo Holder was 14 when the family arrived in Australia. John was a clerk when he enlisted in Subiaco, WA as Pte 2431a in 51st Bn. Australian Infantry. He was killed in action in France when he was nineteen and a half and is remembered on memorial panel 568 HAC Cemetery Ecoust-St Mein. The records show that Harry Holder Snr. states a third son was totally incapacitated in the conflict. A search of the Australian Roll of Honour does not produce details that indicate any of the other brothers were killed.

14] Salisbury, Spr. 16486 Charles N.Z. Engineers. Died of sickness 28th May 1917 aged 32. Husband of Norah A. Salisbury of 18 Newton Road, Auckland.

15] Wishart, Pte 8/4057 Andrew Anderson 1st Bn. Otago Regt. N.Z.E.F. Died 10th July 1917 aged 21. Son of George Blyth & Agnes H.M. Wishart of Makarewa, Invercargill.

16] Protheroe, Dvr 6/3133 William N.Z. Army Service Corps. Died of sickness 15th July 1917 aged 38. Son of Alexander Protheroe of Elgin, Ashburton, Christchurch.

17] Holland, Pte 28885 Francis Arthur Auckland Regt. N.Z.E.F. Died 6th September 1917 aged 30. Son of Matthew & Elizabeth Holland of High Street, Maryborough, Victoria, Australia.

18] Keys, Rfn 32346 Frederick Charles 3rd N.Z. [Rifle] Brigade. Died of sickness 15th April 1917 aged 35. Son of Benjamin Hunt Keys & Annie Jane Keys of 94 Marine Parade, Napier.

19] Dumbleton, Cpl. 8/2901 Ronald Otago Regt. N.Z.E.F. Died of sickness 5th April 1917 aged 26. Son of William & Lucy A. Dumbleton of Pukeuri, Junction, Oamaru.

20] Browning, Pte 34797 Frederick Henry Otago Regt. N.Z.E.F. Died of sickness 31st March 1917 aged 33. Son of John & the late Mrs Browning.

21] **Watson, Pte 31568 Walter Robert** Canterbury Regt. N.Z.E.F. Died of pneumonia 20th March 1917 aged 27. Son of Edward Wilfred & Eliza Watson; husband of Beatrice E. Watson of Fox Hill, Nelson.

22] **McDonald, Pte 28186 Gordon** Wellington Regt. N.Z.E.F. Died of meningitis 5th March 1917 aged 25. Son of John & Ellen McDonald of Te-Ore, Pongaroa, Wellington.

23] **Allen, Pte 31453 William** Canterbury Regt. N.Z.E.F. Died of sickness 23rd February 1917 aged 29. Son of Joseph Allen of Bexley, Canterbury.

24] **Tombs, Pte 31552 Charles** Canterbury Regt. N.Z.E.F. Died 17th February 1917 aged 43. Son of Job & Elizabeth Tombs; born at Sefton, Canterbury.

25] **Delaney, Pte 32149 J.** N.Z. [Rifle] Brigade. Died 17th February 1917.

26] **Button, Corp. 1870 Albert James** 51st Bn. Australian Infantry. Accidentally killed 23rd November 1916 aged 23 or 24. Born Melbourne; enlisted Fremantle WA; worked as a hotel clerk. [b]

27] **Smith, Pte 2782 Michael** 45th Bn. Australian Infantry. Died 5th December 1916 aged 38.

28] **Osborne, Pte 2696 T.E.** 45th Bn Australian Infantry. Died 10th December 1916 aged 33. Both private's Smith and Osborne have crosses as headstones and an inscription: 'Erected by his comrades A Company 12th Training'.

29] **Ryan, Pte 2465 Richard Charles Gladstone** 50th Bn. Australian Infantry. Died of broncho-pneumonia 16th December 1916 aged 21. Son of Richard & Margaret Ina Ryan of Streaky Bay, South Australia; born & enlisted at Talia; worked in farming.

30] **Beattie, Pte 2389 Edwin** 47th Bn Australian Infantry. Died of pneumonia 1st January 1917 aged 22. Son of John & Mary Elizabeth Beattie of Fern Hill, Coomera, Queensland. [c]

31] **Kinane, Pte 2538 Lawrence** 49th Bn Australian Infantry. Died of broncho-pneumonia 6th January 1917 aged 19. Son of Daniel & Catherine Kinane; born in County Cork, Ireland; came to Australia aged 18, worked as a farmer; enlisted Warwick, Queensland.

32] **McGregor, Pte 6621 David Edward** 15th Bn. Australian Infantry. Died of broncho-pneumonia 23rd January 1917 aged 36. Son of Mrs Isabella McGregor; born at Bega, New South Wales; worked as manager of a cheese factory. He had two brothers in the AIF Lieut. McGregor of 121 Light Horse. 'Mentioned in Despatches' & Sgt. Major Wallace McGregor of 25th Battalion 'Military Medal'. Neither man is on the Australian Roll of Honour so it would appear they survived the war.

33] **Brookes, Pte 2628 Harold Vincent** 47th Bn. Australian Infantry. Died of sickness 5th February 1917 aged 19. Son of William & Mary Brookes; born at Ipswich, Queensland.

34] **Parkinson, Pte 7109 Alfred Henry** 16th Bn. Australian Infantry. Died in Sutton Veny Hospital of broncho-pneumonia 26th March 1917 aged 37. Son of William Jones & Isabella Louisa Parkinson; born in

South Australia; worked as a miner as did his brother Pte Charles Frederick Parkinson, 3914, of 11th Battalion. He was killed in action somewhere in France between 22-25th July 1916 aged 30. He is remembered on panel 63 at Villers–Bretonneaux. Inscription reads 'In the path of duty was the way to glory'.

35] **McMullen, Rfn 23416 William** 1st Bn. N.Z. [Rifle] Brigade. Died of sickness 13th February 1917 aged 21. Son of James & Rose McMullen of 20 Arabi St., Mount Albert, Auckland.

36] **Jefferies, Pte 6/2173 Job.** Canterbury Regt. N.Z.E.F. Died 12th February 1917 aged 27. Son of William & Ada Jefferies of Kangahu, Karamea.

37] **Kelland, Pte 31294 John Bodley** Wellington Regt. N.Z.E.F. Died of sickness 11th February 1917 aged 21. Son of George & Mary Kelland of Manaia, Waimate West.

38] **Boland, Pte 26982 Edward James** Canterbury Regt. N.Z.E.F. Died 4th February 1917 aged 31. Son of Francis & Annie Boland of Darfield; husband of Nellie Bolland of Darfield, Christchurch.

39] **Winterburn, Rfn 28568 Betram** N.Z.[Rifle] Brigade. Died of sickness 4th February 1917 aged 40. Son of Arthur A. Winterburn of Tory St., Nelson.

40] **Telford, Rfn 13132 Thomas** 3rd Bn. 3rd N.Z. Rifle Brigade. Died 2nd February 1917 aged 44. Son of James & Mary Telford of Baccus Marsh, Victoria, Australia.

41] **McFarlane, Pte 25284 James Malcolm** Wellington Regt. N.Z.E.F. Died of pneumonia 25th January 1917 aged 23. Son of Peter & Helen McFarlane of 'Hopetoun', Woodgrove, North Canterbury.

42] **Shaw, Pte 27966 Alexander Davison** N.Z. [Rifle] Brigade. Died 15th January 1917 aged 36. Son of Elizabeth Shaw of 170 Coventry Street, South Melbourne & the late Thomas Shaw; born at Sandford, Victoria.

43] **McCloud, Pte 8/2084 James** Otago Regt. N.Z.E.F. Died of sickness 28th December 1916 aged 23. Son of Samuel McCloud of Papatahi, Featherstone, Wellington.

44] **Garlick, Rfn William 17708.** N.Z. [Rifle] Brigade. Died 13th December 1916 aged 29. Son of Charles & Maria Dorothy Garlick of Taneatua, Bay of Plenty.

45] **Glastonbury, Rfn. 25860 Alfred George** N.Z. [Rifle] Brigade. Died 5th December 1916 aged 34. Husband of Mrs M.A. Glastonbury of Ohingaiti.

46] **Darch, Pte 87276 A.J.** 'F'Coy. Royal Army Medical Corps. Died 25th November 1916.

47] **Foster, Rfn 20134 Edward** N.Z. [Rifle] Brigade. Died of sickness 14th November 1916 aged 34.

48] **Pollock, Pte 3587 Alexander** 57th Bn. Australian Infantry. Died 21st February 1919. Enlisted Derby, Victoria.

49] **Ziesler, Cpl 3961 Charles.** 51st Bn. Australian Infantry. Died of sickness in No 3 New Zealand General Hospital 26th June 1918 aged 46. Son of William & Lucy Ziesler; husband of M.M. Ziesler of 68 Outram Street, Perth; born in England.

50] **Clarke, Pte 3762 Sydney James** 49th Bn. Australian Infantry. Died of broncho-pneumonia 21st June 1918 aged 28. Foster son of Mrs. E. Noud of Goondiwindi, Queensland; born & enlisted at St George, Queensland.

51] **Cattermole, Pte 3861 Frank James** 48th Bn. Australian Infantry. Died of sickness 14th June 1918 aged 19. Son of William James & Amelia Jane Cattermole of Bordertown, South Australia; born in Victoria.

52] **Chilton, Pte 1588 Thomas William [also listed as John William Auton]** 53rd Bn. Australian Infantry. Died of sickness 30th March 1918 aged 29. Son of Mrs Sarah Ellen Chilton; born at Ripon, Yorkshire, England. He seems to have been a farmer who arrived in Australia when he was 22 and enlisted in Coolamon NSW. He had been wounded at Suvla Bay in 1914 and in France in 1917.

53] **Jennings, Pte 3861 Clarence Albert** 32nd Bn. Australian Infantry. Died of measles & purulent bronchitis 22nd March 1918 aged 21. Son of Robert Edward & Mary Ann Carrison Jennings of Port MacDonnell, South Australia.

54] **Stratford, Pte 5117 Henry Thomas** 31st Bn. Australian Infantry. Died 4th March 1918. Enlisted in Brisbane; worked as a labourer.

55] **Cameron, Pte 3367 Oscar** 59th Bn. Australian Infantry. Died of chronic nephritis 24th January 1918 aged 37. Son of Christopher & Agnes Cameron of Shelburne, Nova Scotia, Canada.

56] **Cathcart, Pte 7716 William Rea** 16th Bn. Australian Infantry. Died of diabetes 25th November 1917 aged 30. Son of Thomas Cathcart of Windsor Terrace, Ballymena, Co. Antrim, Ireland. Went to Australia at the age of 24; worked as a book-keeper; enlisted in Perth WA.

57] **Bourke, Pte 51681 Walter Edward** Auckland Regt., N.Z.E.F. Died 25th October 1917 aged 36. Son of Eliza & the late Patrick Bourke of 35 Esplanade, Mount Eden, Auckland. Born at Dargaville.

58] **Kearse, Pte 6/2382 Thomas Walker** Canterbury Regt. N.Z.E.F. Died 25th October 1917 aged 23. Husband of Mrs. C. L. Asselin [formerly Kearse] of 25 Holmwood Street, Newtown, Sydney, New South Wales.

59] **Holmes, Pte 23/2204 Arthur** N.Z. Maori [Pioneer] Battalion. Died of sickness 28th December 1917 aged 33.

60] **Whitelaw, Pte 37903 Alexander George** Canterbury Regt., N.Z.E.F. Died of pneumonia 10th January 1918 aged 36. Son of Peter & Agnes Whitelaw of Makarewa, Invercargil; born in Scotland.

61] **Thomas, Rfn 26207 Samuel** 1st Bn. 3rd N.Z. [Rifle] Brigade. Died 14th January 1918 aged 21.

62] **Alley, Pte 10287 Francis Lignori** Otago Regt. N.Z.E.F. Died of sickness 2nd February 1918 aged 22. Son of John & Elizabeth Alley of Salisbury Road, Gisborne.

63] **Moody, Pte 62358 Francis Robert** Canterbury Regt., N.Z.E.F. Died of phthisis 22nd February 1918 aged 31. Son of Francis Rolfe & Mary Moody of Kihi Kihi, Waikato.

64] **Charleston, Rfn 33301 John** N.Z. [Rifle] Brigade. Died of meningitis 15th March 1918 aged 39. Son of John Charles & Clare Charleston of Cardiff, Wales; husband of F. Charleston of 109 Aro Street, Wellington.

65] **Morris, Pte 64558 Frank Kemp** Otago Regt., N.Z.E.F. Died of bronchitis 20th April 1918 aged 32.

66] **Perwick, Pte 39307 Thomas Patrick** Otago Regt., N.Z.E.F. Died 4th May 1918 aged 28. Son of Alfred & Catherine Perwick of St Patrick's, Balfour, Southland.

67] **Harvey, Pte 40212 Charles John** 2nd Coy. 2nd Bn. Canterbury Regt. N.Z.E.F. Died of nephritis 7th May 1918 aged 25. Son of George & Eleonora Margaret Dorothy Harvey of Sandy Bay, Riwaka, Nelson.

68] **O'Neill, Pte 30449 Patrick Thomas** N.Z. Machine Gun Battalion. Died of sickness 23rd May 1918. Son of Mrs Jane and the late Mr O'Neill of 151 Taranaki St., Wellington.

69] **Tucker, Pte 10899 Harry Edward** Wellington Regt., N.Z.E.F. Died of sickness 15th June 1918 aged 26. Son of John Tucker of Weardale Orchard, Havelock North.

70] **Dunne, Serjt 13890 William Patrick** Otago Regt., N.Z.E.F. Died of sickness 19th June 1918 aged 31. Son of Patrick & C. Dunne of Totaratahi, Oamaru.

71] **Moore, Pte 79989 John** Canterbury Regt., N.Z.E.F. Died of pneumonia 13th April 1919 aged 37. Son of Thomas & Helen Moore of Sumner, Christchurch; husband of Mary Moore of 13 High Street, Kaiapoi, Canterbury.

72] **Hape, Pte 16/536 Hona** N.Z. Maori [Pioneer] Battalion. Died of sickness 11th April 1919 aged 26. Son of Hope & Hera Inumia Tangiora of Opoutama, Napier.

73] **Gilmour, Cpl. 10/3886 William** N.Z. Medical Corps. Died of influenza 7th April 1919 aged 52. Youngest son of the late John & Isabella Gilmour of New Plymouth.

74] **Kearse, Rfn 25/1771 Bertie Ernest** 1st Bn. 3rd N.Z. [Rifle] Brigade. Died of sickness 16th July 1918 aged 40. Son of Thomas F. Kearse of 15 Owen Street, Wellington; husband of the late Ada Kearse. Born at Wanganui.

75] **Hayes, Pte 63153 Daniel** Otago Regt. N.Z.E.F. Died of pneumonia 31st March 1919 aged 24. Son of Ann & the late John Hayes of Outram, Dunedin.

76] **Aicken, Rfn 72925 William Michael** N.Z.[Rifle] Brigade. Died of pneumonia 28th March 1919 aged 27. Son of William & Jessie Aicken of Aickens, Westland.

77] **Freitas, Pte 47553 David** Canterbury Regt. N.Z.E.F. Died of sickness 21st February 1919 aged 35. Son of Mr F. & Mrs M.A. Freitas of Three Mile, Hokitika.

78] **Sexton, Rfn. 65462 Michael** N.Z. [Rifle] Brigade. Died 18th February 1919 aged 30. Son of William & Bridget Sexton of Westport.

79] **Hayes, QMS [W.O.II] 5/242B Charles William** N.Z. Army Service Corps. Died of pneumonia 16th February1919 aged 34. Son of Porter Theodore & Elizabeth Hayes of Auckland; husband of Emily Hayes of 25b Hanson Street, Newtown, Wellington.

80] **Maley, Lce Cpl 8/3001 Archibald James** 1st Bn. Otago Regt., N.Z.E.F. Died 15th February 1919 aged 24; born at Mataura.

81] **Wakelin, Capt 6/2891 William Richard** Canterbury Regt., N.Z.E.F. Died 5th February 1919 . Eldest son of Mrs G.A. & the late G.K. Wakelin of Blenheim.

82] **Griffin, Pte 81179 Alexander John** Otago Regt. N.Z.E.F. Died of sickness 22nd January 1919 aged 29. Husband of Mrs E.M. Griffin of Bonny Glen, Marton, Wanganui.

83] **Jordan, Major 6/1109 Benjamin Stevens** Canterbury Regt. N.Z.E.F. Died of accidental injuries in a plane crash 24th May 1918 aged 34. Son of Mr S & the late Ellen Jordan of Rangiora; husband of Elsie C. Jordan of 136 Bishop Street, St Albans, Christchurch. [d]

84] **King, Pte 16761 Walter Edward** Auckland Regt. N.Z.E.F. Died 14th December 1918 aged 27. Son of John Henry & Johannah Augusta King of North Loburn, Canterbury.

85] **McDonnell, Pte 17806 James William** 1st Bn. Canterbury Regt., N.Z.E.F. Died of pneumonia 18th November 1918 aged 27. Son of Eliza Amy & the late William McDonnell of 97 Barbour Street, Linwood, Christchurch.

86] **O'Connor, Pte 60184 Graham Wakefield** Auckland Regt., N.Z.E.F. Died of pneumonia, 9th November 1918 aged 24. Only son of Charles & Ellen Nina O'Conner of 28 Omahu Road, Remuera, Auckland; born at Christchurch.

87] **Mincher, Pte 26885 Oswold Alan** 2nd Bn. Auckland Regt. N.Z.E.F. Died on pneumonia 15th November 1918 aged 30. Son of James & Elizabeth Mincher of Northcote, Auckland.

88] **Guthrie, Rfn 57070 William George** 3rd Bn 3rd N.Z. [Rifle] Brigade. Died of pneumonia 29th October 1918 aged 40. Son of William & Jane Guthrie of Havelock North, Napier.

89] **Byrne, Lce Cpl 4/535 Vincent John** N.Z. Engineers. Died 19th October 1918 aged 27. Son of Thomas Vincent & Frances A.M. Byrne of Kumara, Westland.

90] **Saville, Pte 73523 John George** New Zealand Reinforcement. Died of bronchitis 15th September 1918 aged 30. Son of Frank & Sarah Saville; husband of H.J. Saville of 13 Craighead Street, Timaru. Born in Durham, England.

91] **Elton, Pte 38792 Charles Edward Stuart** Wellington Regt. N.Z.E.F. Died of sickness 15th September 1918 aged 25. Son of Arthur & Elizabeth Elton of 207 Coutts Street, Kilbirnie South, Wellington.

92] **McEnteer, Pte 76955 Claude** "E" Coy. 40th New Zealand Reinforcements. Died of bronchitis 13th September 1918 aged 20. Son of James & Elizabeth McEnteer of Grey Street, Waihi; born at Thames.

93] **Pilkington, Pte 75251 Zell Eric Ivon** Machine Gun Sect., 40th New Zealand Reinforcements. Died of pneumonia 12th September 1918 aged 20. Son of Mr. W.A. & Mrs E.D.B. Pilkington of 1 Grey Street, Devonport, Auckland.

94] **Magee, Pte 52446 Joseph** Auckland Regt., N.Z.E.F. Died of sickness 2nd September 1918 aged 40. Son of late James & Mary Ann Magee of Ireland.

95] **Stevenson, Pte 11587 Bertram Onslow** N.Z. Medical Corps. Died of meningitis 24th July 1918 aged 36.

96] **Wade, Pte 61006 John** Canterbury Regt. N.Z.E.F. Died of phthisis 23rd August 1918 aged 34. Son of John E and C Wade of Winchester Road, Temuka, Canterbury.

97] **Westerby, Pte 75618 William James** N.Z. Medical Corps. Died of sickness 30th August 1918 aged 30. Husband of Lillie M. Munn [formerly Westerby] of Greytown, Wellington.

98] **Nicolson, Pte 29844 Archibald John** Otago Regt. N.Z.E.F. Died of pneumonia 14th July 1918 aged 23. Son of Donald & Isabella McDonald Nicolson of Deveraux Road, Winton, Southland.

This beautiful and peaceful cemetery is today a place of pilgrimage, it is also a place to reflect on the tragedy of so many young men who arrived in the vigour of youth and never returned to their loved ones. Pneumonia and sickness accounted for the majority of the deaths, 56 that we know of. Very few of the men seem to have been married.

a] Private Albert Arthur Harris known to his parents as 'Sonnie' was the eldest son of Arthur and Eliza Harris; he came from Ranelagh in the Huon Valley and was an orchardist with a passion for horses. His sweetheart Amy became pregnant with their son Reginald before he left to fight; Sonnie was never to see his child, he died of peritonitis as a result of bullet wounds received in Malta in 1917. Machine gun crews were the target of every enemy weapon on the battlefield; the officers and men of the British Machine Gun Corps were nicknamed 'The Suicide Club' with a casualty rate in excess of 33%. Reg knew very little about his father, he was orphaned at 16 when his mother died; Amy had never married.

'Sonnie' Harris

b] Corporal Button was killed in a training accident at No. 2 Camp Codford, when a live grenade thrown by Private Taylor of 51st Bn. landed in a bay full of men waiting their turn to practice. The other men escaped almost unscathed; Corporal Button froze, he was seriously injured and died before reaching hospital. At the Inquest it was recorded that "A grenade fragment had passed completely through his brain, death being due to a fracture of the skull. Deceased had a few wounds on his legs but they were quite slight."

Grenades were only responsible for 2% of the British casualties in WWI. Mortar bombs and shells accounted for 58.7%, bullets 39% and bayonets 0.3%

c] Private Edwin Beattie Edwin Beattie was born in Coomera, Queensland in 1894 to John and Mary Elizabeth Beattie [nee Harding]. He was a twenty-two year old farmer when he enlisted with the 47th Infantry, 5th Reinforcements of the Australian Army on 28th March 1916. His older brother George aged twenty-seven enlisted on the same day, both brothers embarked from Brisbane on the Seang Choon on 19th September 1916 and disembarked at Plymouth on 9th December 1916.

Reinforcements were only given basic training in Australia. Training was completed in training units in England located on Salisbury Plain and other nearby areas in Wiltshire. Edwin was admitted to Devonport Hospital from HMAT Seang Choon on 9th December 1916- sick [slight] with mumps. He was transferred to the military hospital at Sutton Veny Wiltshire on 23rd December diagnosed with influenza. He developed signs of pneumonia on 24th December 1916. Edwin Beattie died of pneumonia at 7.55pm on 1st January 1917 and was buried at 2pm on 3rd January 1917

Edwin Beattie

Note: Pte 2389 George Beattie was killed in action in the Battle of Albert on 28th March 1918 aged twenty-nine. He is remembered on Villiers-Brettoneux Memorial as he has no known grave.

Pte Edwin Beattie & his brother Pte George Beattie are both remembered on their father's headstone located at Lower Coomera Cemetery, Queensland, Australia

d] Major Benjamin Jordan *at the time of his death on Friday 24th May 1918, was second in command of the New Zealand Command Depot at Codford. He was a passenger on an Airco DH6C6518 piloted by 2nd Lieutenant Joseph J. Daley from New York based at No 8 Training Depot Station at Netheravon. The crash occurred when the outer port wings collapsed as the aircraft began to pull out of a loop and dive manoeuvre to 1000 feet. The Training Depot had been formed 1st April that year and was responsible for basic and advanced training; the crash was its first fatality.*

The Men in Commonwealth War Grave [ANZAC] Cemetery
66 New Zealanders & 31 Australians

When the war ended families from the antipodes were asked to fill in forms listing the cause of death of the men in the ANZAC War Graves. Only 68 families responded so we have no personal information for 29 of the men. Virulent strains of influenza, bronchitis, measles and meningitis were early twentieth century plagues. The Spanish Flu pandemic accounted for many casualties during The Great War. However only 2 men in the cemetery are recorded as dying of influenza. During 1918 and until April of 1919 many casualties are listed as dying of pneumonia. The majority died during 1917 - 1918 with the most common cause of death listed as 'sickness.'

Cause of death where known:

Sickness	28
Pneumonia	18
Broncho-pneumonia	6
Bronchitis	5
Meningitis	4
Influenza	2
Phthisis [pulmonary consumption]	2
Nephritis [inflammation of the kidney]	2
Wounds	1
Training accident	1
Plane Crash	1
Diabetes	1
Measles & purulent bronchitis	1

Age at death	Number	Year of death	Number
19	4	1916	9
20's	39	1917	43
30's	34	1918	34
40's	8	1919	12
52	1		

Lance Serjeant, 2732759 Christopher Thomas Brown

The single grave from WWII is sited near the Cross of Sacrifice, close to the hedge bordering Church Lane beneath a large Beech tree. Thirty-three year old Lance Serjeant Christopher Thomas Brown was in the 2nd Battalion Welsh Guards stationed at Codford with 6th Guards Armoured Tank Brigade. Born on 29th August 1909, the son of William Telford and Elizabeth Brown; Christopher Brown enlisted in Middlesborough eight days before his eighteenth birthday on 21st August 1928. From 1929-1930 he served in Egypt, transferring to the reserves two years later. He was recalled to regular service in 1939, promoted to Lance Corporal on 17th June 1940 and to Lance Serjeant three months later.

Christopher Brown was found dead of gunshot wounds to the head in the room adjoining the Serjeants Mess on 8th April 1942. His head was laid on a kit bag and there was a rifle on the floor by his side, medical evidence at the inquest stated that the skin around the wound was discoloured by explosive and the shot had penetrated the brain. He left a widow, Elizabeth Doris, and two sons who were living at this time in Penberth, Cornwall.

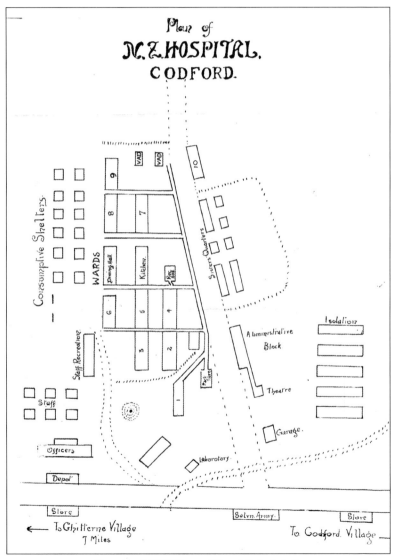

Plan curtesy of RNZAMC Museum - Chitterne to Codford is 3 miles

ANZAC REQUIEM

On this day above all others we recall those who served in war and did not return to receive the grateful thanks of the nation. We remember those who are still where they were left; amid the scrub in the valleys and the ridges of Gallipoli; on the rocky and terraced hills of Palestine and in the cemeteries of France.

We remember those that lie in ground beneath the shimmering haze of the Libyan Desert. At Bardia, Derna and Tobruk, and amid the mountain passes and olive groves of Greece and Crete, and the rugged hills of Syria and Lebanon.

We remember those who lie buried in the jungles of Malaysia, Singapore and Burma. In New Guinea and in the islands of the Pacific.

We remember those who lie buried amid loving friends in Great Britain and in unknown resting places in almost every land and those gallant men whose grave is the unending sea.

We remember those who died as prisoners of war, remote from their homeland.

We think of those members of the women's services who gave their lives for ours in foreign lands and at sea.

We recall too, the staunch friends who fought beside us on the first ANZAC Day and ever since- men of New Zealand – who helped create the name of ANZAC.

We think of every man and woman who in the crucial hours of World War Two died so that the light of freedom and humanity might continue to shine.

We think of those gallant men who died in Korea, in Malaya and in Vietnam and in the pursuit of peace since then.

May they rest in the knowledge of their achievement and may we- and our successors in that heritage- prove worthy of their sacrifice.

Lest we forget.

Lone Pine Cemetery & Memorial in Gallipoli [Gelibolu]
The Memorial commemorates more than 4,900 Australian & New Zealand Servicemen who died in the ANZAC area whose graves are not known . Others named on the Memorial were buried at sea.

The Codford Badge

The Codford Badge hill figure also known as The Australian Badge or The Rising Sun is situated on Lamb Down, a steep hillside facing south towards the Wylye Valley at the eastern end of the village. In its original form it depicted a Trophy of Arms- the Badge of the Australian Imperial Force. The 175 by 150 foot Badge was cut into the chalk in 1916 after the Australian Brigade Commander, looking at the hill from his HQ at Stockton House in Stockton decided that defaulters should be made as part of their punishment to carve the Badge in this prominent position. The soldiers having to march up and down the hill in full kit and climb up for physical training often in bitter conditions nicknamed the site 'Misery Hill.' Another name commonly used locally was 'The Pimple.'

Present day Codford Badge on Lamb Down

ANZAC Cove Gallipoli

Gallipoli/Gelibolu across the Dardenelles

ANZAC Cemetery from St Mary's Church Tower

Sources:

Brendan Hall - Genealogical Society of Ireland Vol 14

The Commonwealth War Graves Commission

'Brassey's Battles' by John Laffin

Col Sir William Mahon LVO

Brigadier Simon Firth CBE

David Read - Soldiers of Gloucestershire Museum

Kay Stephenson - Durham Light Infantry Museum

Kate Swann - National Army Museum

Rob McIntosh - Army Medical Services Museum

Steve Fuller - The Bedfordshire Regiment in the Great War

Chris Bacon - The Wiltshire Regiment at The Wardrobe

Cathy Sedgwick - Wiltshire OPC Project

Matt Beales

Andrew Frostick

Georgena Kemp

'Swords and Ploughshares - Codford During the 20th Century'- Romy Wyeth

'Warriors For The Working Day - Codford During Two World Wars'- Romy Wyeth